Devon Rex as Pets

A Care Guide for Devon Rex Cats

Devon Rex Cat General Info, Purchasing, Care, Cost, Keeping, Health, Supplies, Food, Breeding and More Included!

By Lolly Brown

Copyrights and Trademarks

Disclaimer and Legal Notice

Foreword

There are so many reasons why people are drawn to this breed and the countless reason is clear. Not only does the Devon Rex have a stunning physique that is both lithe and graceful, allowing it easy movements, it also has unique characteristics that endear itself to its caregivers. The Devon Rex is a remarkable feline, who has a playful nature and a high level of intelligence. It has been one cat that has been sought after by cat aficionados all over because it is said that the Devon Rex is one perfect companion to have around the house.

The devon rex loves it when it is shown attention and given affection by its human wards. It loves being patted tenderly, adoring how you stroke it. It appreciates the gentle talk you share with it and would sometimes respond to your chatter. It absolutely dotes on the attention it is given by its caregivers, friends and family.

Table of Contents

Chapter One: Presenting the Devon Rex Cat

Households who possess existing feline pets have been known to welcome a Devon Rex without too much fuss, with the proper supervision. You will find that integrating a Devon Rex is not at all difficult to do because it is a friendly little thing that will be curious and inquisitive about its new human (and/or) and other pet companions. It is generally a gentle cat who will want to take time to get to know its new spaces and those who occupy it. If it shows to be a little aloof at first, don't fret. All cats seem a little shy when they are around new people, but this does not mean it will not warm up to you. In fact, a Devon Rex will most likely gravitate toward one or two people in the family more than they would to others. This does not mean they would avoid other people in the family; it's just that the Devon Rex, like most felines, would naturally have a "favorite" human they would be more comfortable being around. The Devon Rex is an openly affectionate feline who can become deeply devoted to their human wards, with no reservations.

The Devon Rex, in all the many glorious color patterns it comes in, is a graceful feline who loves nothing more than to spend time with their beloved family members. It gets along famously well with people who care for them, given enough time and space it needs to get used to its new surroundings and people. Once acclimated into the new household and it has gotten used to the presence of other family members, the Devon Rex will settle in with very little fuss.

The elvish-looking Devon Rex is a sensitive cat who is able to detect mood shifts in their human wards. Sensing the mood changes in their humans signals the Devon Rex to step in and try to help out the humans in whatever situation they are in, in any way they can. It would not be unusual for the cat from Devonshire to mirror their caregiver's moods and inner workings. When it senses anxiety in their humans, the Devon Rex would typically sidle up and snuggle with you to relieve you off of the stress being experienced at any given moment.

This curly-furred cat is truly a loving companion to have around the house, because of its amusing antics and clever sensibilities. It is possessive and protective of their home and owners. Being a keen and clever cat, it likes to check out anyone or anything new introduced to its home environment. It is not at all unusual for the Devon Rex to cozy up to you during downtime. The Devon Rex is happiest when you are around and dotes on the loving attention extended to it by family members. It loves sharing space with its human ward and loves it when you are relaxed.

The devon rex cat is a feline you would want to raise and keep indoors. Being a generally friendly cat, your cat may get too chummy with someone who may want to keep it for themself. Keeping the cat indoors would also prevent unwarranted attacks from bigger animals that may roam your area. Aside from the dangers of street traffic, there is always a chance your devon rex many stray too far from home and not be able to find its way back to you. They are a breed of cats who are gaining great popularity because of their amiable and friendly disposition, so it is strongly advised that you keep your devon rex indoors with occasional, supervised trips outside of the home.

The devon rex likes to sit atop high places in order to survey its terrain from a good vantage point. This vantage point is usually the utmost part of your body. It will make itself comfortable on your shoulder, giving it a head level view of the room around it. It is a cat who takes lively interest in the things that keep its humans busy and would not hear of any talk about keeping to itself. You can be sure that the devon rex will want to be close to you when you are around and will, on occasion, communicate its head musings to you in a sweet, quiet voice.

Chapter Two: History of the Devon Rex

Those who do not know about the Devon Rex's origins would probably weave fantastic tales of how these sweet, elfish-looking felines came about. It is not difficult to see how some would wonder about the Devon Rex. It does seem to have an ethereal quality about them. The devon rex is such an intelligent cat that it has been given many monikers. Since it has a personality and extends loyalty much like a canine would it has been likened to a dog. Others have dubbed the cat from Devonshire, England as a cat in a monkey suit because of its keen smarts. It is not unusual for a devon rex to learn tricks that people would normally think only dogs can learn.

Devon Rex in Focus

Devon Rex cats share particular genetic traits but you will find the joy of getting to know each devon rex and discover how, much like people, diverse they are in moods and personality. It is an inquisitive feline who would shadow and hound you around the house as you go about your usual stuff. Mind your step because the devon rex may just be under foot should you have to retrace your steps. You will often find your devon rex's cat right up your nose when you are busy tinkering about, trying to find ways it can lend you a hand. A vocal little fur-ball, the devon rex would trill, purr, mew, and make all those fancy cat noises that they make. The devon rex, would chime in and give you its two-cents worth if it observes your labor to be a tad lackluster.

Although a generally quiet cat who would just be happy to be around you, when addressed, the devon rex would happily respond. Every cat has their own character and personality, and any cat lover can attest to this fact. You will find they years that follow with your devo rex will be happy years of getting to know each other.

It's been reported that cats have the ability to relieve stress from people; that felines in general are cathartic, almost healing pets who somehow manage to help us "repair" ourselves. There is something almost infectious about having a calm devon rex cat, sit contentedly on your lap. These cats are the sort who almost always needs to be reminded about boundaries and personal space. The devon rex would get into your business and would not think anything of perching on your shoulder as you work at your desk. They are a playful and rambunctious by nature as well. A litter of devon rexs will definitely need to get lots of playtime with you so as to channel all their high energy in positive ways.

Historical Facts about the Devon Rex

Any potential pet owner, whether the pet be of the cold-blooded sort, the winged sort, the slithering or hopping sort or the four-legged sort, should take time to get to know about the pet they are looking to take in and raise to be able to have a greater chance of raising the animal correctly. Get off on the right foot and get to know the Devon Rex and its many traits, needs and personality. A good headstart to welcoming your new devon rex cat home begins with your awareness and preparedness for the road ahead. Since you are in the market for a cat, it would serve you well to know that you are amongst the many millions of cat lovers the world over. Word has it that, in America, there are more cat owners than there are dog owners. Perhaps that is because cats are fairly independent and is able to fare well without too much of a fuss.

The cat, whose ancestor hailed from Devonshire, England, has adorable pixie-like features that are a joy to observe. Its ridiculously large ears are perched on the sides of its head giving it an appearance of having butterfly wings. The devon rex has big huge eyes that would stare at you lovingly and are set on a tiny face with high cheekbones. It is a breed of cat that came about in 1959 at a London town called Devonshire and was fathered by a roaming Tom. The first devon rex introduced to the United States came about in 1968 and the popularity of the breed has not wavered since then. It didn't take long for Cat Fanciers Association to sit up and take notice of the curious looking, elfish-like cat, and gave it full recognition in 1979. The cat comes in many color patterns from white, black, blue, chocolate, cinnamon, lavender and various combinations and patterns. It weighs about 5 to 10 pounds and has a lifespan of 15 years. It has a moderate activity level coupled with high intelligence. Provide it with physically and mentally stimulating toys because it enjoys play time like a boss.

Devon rex cats will not think twice about sitting with you at the table for meals and would probably think that you had prepared the meal for them. Be careful that you keep away any meant-for-human foods hidden away until it is actually meal time for the family because the devon rex will help himself to it otherwise. It has a hardy appetite and will not think twice about asking for more. You will want to monitor the amount and portions of food you feed it since it does take on to food with great gusto. Bed time is another favorite time of the devon rex and it always manages to find the warmest and safest spot to get its z's - beside you and under the covers. We were not kidding when we said this cat has no sense of personal space. Anywhere you are seems to be their preferred lounging area.

It is a moderately active, cheeky and mischievous cat who possesses endearing qualities which are easy to warm up to. There is always something interesting going on in the life of a devon rex and it will surely want to include you.

Chapter Three: Devon Rex Requirements

The Devon Rex Cat is a pretty robust feline in comparison to other pedigreed cat breeds. They are prone to a few conditions that can either be avoided, or managed through proper care and nurturing. As long as particular conditions are met in order for them to thrive in a healthy environment, the devon rex will stay healthy and their usual pleasant selves. They require little but the routine care and grooming that should be carried out to maintain their health and wellness. We shall be discussing the needs of the playfully cute Devon Rex. We shall also discuss what is expected of any one who intends to get a new cat as well as the pros and cons of raising one.

You will also be able to find out if keeping more than one of these lovely cats is possible. Find out how much purchasing or adopting one would set you back initially, and get an idea of how much you will be spending for its maintenance and upkeep on a monthly and annual basis. We have included a run - down of costs you will be incurring upon acquisition of a Devon Rex and how much you are looking at on a monthly basis.

Pros and Cons of Devon Rex Cats

The Devon Rex Cat is generally lauded one of the healthiest of felines amongst most, if not all, cat sorts. All cats are prone to developing health problems, just as easily as a human would inherit a disease. An upstanding breeder would cannot claim that a cat is free of genetic or health problems. Do not do business with anyone who says otherwise. The great ancestor of the cat from the English county of Devonshire is an overall healthy cat with a minor probability, given the right attention and care, of a few ailments. Make sure that the breeder you do business with will be able to hand over solid, paper based health guarantee for the devon rex kitten.

Hypertrophic cardiomyopathy (HCM) is a typical form of heart disease seen in cats. This heart disease causes hypertrophy, a thickening of the heart muscle. A vet would be able to confirm this by ordering an echocardiogram which can confirm if a feline has HCM. You will want to cross out breeders from your lists who claim to have HCM-free kittens in their breed. No one can give any sort of guarantee that the felines under their care will never develop the condition. Devon Rexes that result from breeding must be examined and tested for HCM. If a cat is found to be associated with HCM, the devon rex must be taken out from breeding programs. Make sure that the breeding pair or the parents of the kitten you are acquiring have both been tested for HCM, supported by documentation.

No matter what sort of pet you decide to take in, make sure that you research possible illnesses and to which your pet may be prone. Doing so prior to bringing one home saves you for unexpected surprises and allows you to set reasonable expectations for when you take home with your new feline companion. Make this a priority at the onset of your decision to take in one. This will be important to your success in raising the cat correctly.

A hereditary problem which may require surgical correction is patellar luxation. This genetically passed on condition involves the popping out of the cat's kneecap. This condition would cause the cat to limp or hop when in movement. The condition usually corrects itself and the kneecap pops back into place on its own. However there are some cases which are more severe than others and would require you to take in your feline friend for surgery.

You will have to do a lot of calling, asking questions and studying to empower yourself to know all you need to know about the background, history, breeding methods and possible medical conditions an animal may be averse to and prone. Whenever taking in a new pet it is but wise and sound to discuss possible illnesses your pet may contract with a pet health care provider - namely, your vet. You, as its caregiver, will have to study up on what to avoid keeping your cat safe and healthy.

Needless to say, you will need to do some investigative digging by doing the proper research on the needs of your devon rex, and that is why you are here. When you have determined certain people you will be talking to down the road of acquiring a devon rex, whether you go to a shelter, talk to a breeder or adopt, asking questions, being present and observant will lead you to a good pairing for you and the cat. Make yourself aware of the history as well as the needs of the cat, so that you in turn can determine if you are up for the union.

Make sure that you get all the necessary equipment and sundries your devon rex cat will need to keep itself occupied and engaged whilst you are away. If you are the sort of owner who spends their day at a job away from home, you may want to consider getting a pair of cats from the same litter. Although relatively independent, the devon rex thrives best with company around, yours in particular. If this can't be avoided then there are other options you may consider. You will, all the more, want to provide your devon orex cats with toys and devices that wouldn't keep them from turning your house into a playground and your furniture and ornaments into playthings. Just make sure that when you are in the house, you spend lots of quality time with your cats, playing and interacting with them.

Ask for vet recommendations from friends and community members who have pets. It is important that you coordinate, consult with and have a vet you can call on, not only for emergencies, mind you! Even before acquiring your pet, you will want to consult with your vet and find out more about the pet you intend to take in. Your vet will be an important resource of information about the health and possible conditions your pet may acquire. They will be the best people to give you advice on what sort of nutrition your pet will need. They will also be the best candidates to identify illness or malaise in the animal. Make sure that you have a trusted vet on your speed dial.

This feline from England is a playful breed with a notably high level of intelligence and of moderate activity.

The devon rex isn't one who would go into overdrive when too excited, so you won't have to deal with an overly hyperactive cat mate if you have your heart set on bringing home a devon rex. This is one cat that knows how to have fun and is one heck of a great playmate.

Behavior with Children and Other Pets

Most children love pets and it will not be unusual for parents to hear their children ask for pets to keep and raise. Not only does a pet help the child learn to take responsibilities that are age appropriate to their abilities, keeping animals as pets also allows children to learn about individual personalities and life in general.

Owning a devon rex is especially fun because it is an amazing little cat who will go well and be great friends with children. It will be hard to resist falling in love with one of these pixie-faced little purring machines once you get to see and know them. It has a really tiny face marked by big expressive eyes and comically large ears. They are an intelligent sort of pet who not only has one of the cutest looks in the cat spectrum, their innate intelligence is also one characteristic of the devon rex that you will impress you.

They are generally friendly and not at all snooty or stand offish. In fact they are really fun cats who have no idea about personal space. They are the sort of cats who would not only gladly hop up on the table during meal times and would love nothing but to join you to feast, they would also want to curl up and sleep with you. They are not the sort of cats who would tolerate a bit of loving from you then jump off and scamper off somewhere.

Let everyone in the family understand and employ proper handling of the devon rex. Teach and show little children the right way to handle the cat and that just like them, respect is very important in any relationship.

It will tolerate and put up with the handling of clumsy toddlers. It almost seems as if the devon rex recognizes that there is no harm meant. You and the cat will always know when it is too much and they may tend to walk away or stay out of reach of people who may handle them a little too clumsily. Make it a point to supervise all interaction with smaller toddlers and children. This will soon enough change when everyone has settled.

You will see that as time passed both the child and the cat would gain confidence in its surroundings and develops trust toward each other. It will sometimes be hard to tear them apart, say when school time comes around. The devon rex is a cat who you will recognize to be a kitten in a cat suit as the years go by. The devon rex tends to stay a kitten way after it has matured. They are loving pets who love nothing more than to spend play time with the little ones.

The Russian Blue is open and accepting of other pets, including cat-friendly canines, so long as they are not menaced, chased or harassed by them. It is strongly advised that introduction of pets be done in a slow and controlled environment, ideally with another caregiver present, to ensure they are given time to get used to each other, and also by giving them enough time, room and space to learn to get along.

A great seeker of attention, it is safe to say that the devon rex stays a kitten at heart during its lifetime. It isn't the type to lose its sweet nature and its love for play no matter what age it is. It stays a cheeky kitten even in maturity and be accomplice to children who sneak them food under the table. The devon rex is also a happy eater and will gladly accept that healthy green colored yummy which your mum keeps telling you is good for you.

It would seem they are great magicians who, even after a proper feeding, would excitedly gobble up anything offered to it. Such a hardy eater it is that you will have to hawk-like instincts that would signal your devon rex lurking on your slaved-over 4-course meal.

Teach your kids a bit of responsibility and monitor that they take on some of the jobs needed to be done by pet owner. You can designate feeding the cats to your little children and assist them with feeding portions. They will grow up understanding the importance of extending caring love to others, as well as the importance of proper nutrition and nourishment.

The devon rex is not at all hypo-allergenic, but it does shed far less than your average cat, and even lesser compared to the more thickly-coated cats like angoras. Some people would say that they have far less reactions and issues with a devon rex than they would with other cats. It is generally a self-sufficient cat who you would only need to groom on occasion since it is typically able to groom itself on its own.

The devon rex is a good pet choice for people who have never owned cats or a big family who has other furry, flighty, scamppery, slithery friends. A small investment of time and patience will be all it would take to successfully integrate your new devon rex into your own brand of home dynamics.

How Many of Them Should You Take In?

Anyone considering one devon rex would fare better if they decided to bring home two of this beautiful breed. Not only do they enjoy your loving and attentive companionship, they also love being around and playing with other pets, no matter what animal they may be. Being raised with another devon rex will be conducive to the cats mental and physical health. Not only would they have the companionship they would need for times when you are out at work.

You will find that you pairing off with a devon rex or two (or three) is almost like a piece of heaven on earth. Not only are cats great sources of stress relief, they are also comical little critters who like to show off their smarts by impressively learning "tricks". Their level of intelligence is such that merely studying you do repeated actions is enough to have them learn some of these actions. Perhaps this is why they are chosen to be shown in the ring.

Ease and Cost of Care of a Devon Rex

The Devon Rex Cat is one of the easiest feline breed to care for and share a home with because of its utterly loving and pleasant demeanor. It is one of the most adorable cats around and they are so easy to live with to boot! The fine-boned, elfin-looking feline with the playful disposition and kitten-like attributes is one cat breed who is so easy to get along with and integrate into the family. This cat has been likened to have the loyal characteristics of dogs, minus the slobbering show of love.

Given the proper attention and given a conducive living environment, devon rexes are hardy little beings who love nothing more than being around you or getting their noses in the things that distract you from their majestic cuteness. They have a fun-loving personality who has no problem spending every waking, and sleeping, moment in your presence. When not trying to get comfortable in the crook of your neck and the ridge of your shoulder, the devon rex will shadow your movements around the house.

A male devon rex would weigh anywhere between 8 to 10 pounds while a female devon rex would weigh in anywhere between 5 to 8 pounds. Aside from being called the name they are known for in the fancy, devon rexes are also called the Pixie Cat, Poodles Cat, and Alien Cat.

It has a soft, silky fur that is both short and curly. The devon rex, is highly interactive as it is loyal. It is social and playful as it loving.

Initial Costs

We pray that you are lucky enough to be friends with someone who is looking to get their kittens adopted into a good home. This is the cheapest route to get a devon rex. You may also check out adopting an adult devon rex or two from the nearest shelter in your locality who has one. Acquisition and cost of living and upkeep of one devon rex kitten will cost you a considerable chunk of money during the first year. So do the wise thing of sorting out your finances early on before the actual introduction of the pet to your home. You wouldn't want to jeopardize any planned vacations or break the bank.

Price of a Devon Rex Kitten

First of all, In terms of finances, the important bit of information you need to know at this time is the average price of a devon rex kitten. You don't want to be taken for a ride and pay more than the actual going rate of a kitten, nor do you want to pay close to nothing and get a sickly cat. The prices will also vary depending on the breeder you will be dealing with. There are some breeders who would hand over spayed and neutered kittens which would have also had the proper medical screenings done and appropriate vaccination. The kittens coming from breeders as these would also have been wormed and have had their rabies shots given. They would also have been tested negative for FeLV/FIV. Of course extras such as the kittens coming with a Kitty Book, carrier, blanket, toys and food would also probably cost more than the average cat.

The average market price of a pet quality devon rex ranges from $350-$400 but this price does not include any of the vaccines or tests that would usually come when dealing with an upstanding breeder. These kittens would not have been given their rabies shot and there would be no assurance that the kitten had not been cut and weaned off suddenly from having their mom's milk. Takin in a devon rex, or any kitten for that matter, that has not had its proper time with to have the nurishment from its mother would make the kitten highly susceptible to all sorts of diseases. You may think you are getting a devon rex for a steal at this price, but this will show to be otherwise in the long run. You may get stuck with a growing pile of medical bills, and this is something you do not want to happen unless you are ready for the responsibility and are actually looking to save a sickly cat.

Kittens that are born of champion lines and are acquired for breeding and showing reasons are even more costly, and the price for one can range anywhere from $800 - $3000 for each kitten.

Shipping Costs

Shipping fees, if you are getting the kitten from out of state, has to be factored into the initial costs. This will be a considerable amount, and a varying one, depending on how far away you live from the breeder. Since the Devon Rex is quite a unique breed of feline, you may possibly have to order your Devon Rex kitten outside of your home state or country. Shipping one to you usually costs around $150-$250. There are breeders who also charge shipping crates, vaccinations and health certificates.

To find out about this, you want to get in touch with shipping and handling company to ask about its shipping prices for pets. Shipping and handling fees will also be depedent on the location of origin.

Supplies

Some Devon Rex breeders will be happy to give you little extras like toys, blankets, feeding dishes, and foods your devon rex used while nursing under their care. However, if the devon rex is being sent in from a far off location, these things will have to be counted into the shipping costs.

Here are other things you will have to get and prepare for before you welcome your new furry friendly to your home:

- Bed and blankets: $25 - $75
- Kitten Food: $15-$30
- Treats: $5 - $15
- Feeders and bowls: $50 - $150
- Collar, Harness and/or Leash: $5 - $20
- Brush: $4 - $50
- Trimmers and Clippers: $6 - $50
- Litter: $5 - $35
- Litter Boxes: $15 - $200
- Waste Disposal: $3 - $30
- Filters and deodorants: $4 - $25
- Liners and mats: $2 - $40
- Toys: $1 - $50
- Toy Crate: $10 - $150
- Cat carrier: $25 - $200
- Vaccination for kittens: $50 - $100
- Vet visit: $35 - $50

The prices of each of these items will largely depend on your taste, as well as the quality of the product. Since you will be spending countless joyful years with your cat, you are advised to put your money on sturdy well-made equipment and sundries that will last for the long haul. You will also want to get the recommendation of the breeder about the sort of food that will be suitable and healthy for your devon rex.

Monthly Costs

The expenses will taper off to a comfortable minimum after you have welcomed the cat into your home. Expenses will be more stable and be more consistent. Since you have already supplied it with the initial and necessary equipment and sundries, monthly expenses will now only be spent on food and treats.

In order not to be stuck with paying for expenses your income cannot afford get your finances sorted out for the monthly care of your devon rex. Here is a quick look at what you should expect to spend each month:

- Kitten Food: $15-$30
- Treats: $5 - $15
- Litter: $5 - $35
- Waste Disposal: $3 - $30
- Filters and deodorants: $4 - $25

- Liners and mats: $2 - $40

Chapter Four: Tips in Buying Devon Rex Cats

The first order of business in buying a devon rex is finding a reputable breeder who has had recent success in breeding devon rexs. Dealing with an upstanding and well-known breeder of devon rexs is one way to determine the health conditions of the kitten you will be getting. The devon rex in general is a healthy, hardy and robust feline who has been blessed with the good fortune of overall good health. However, you should still be mindful of where you are getting the cat from and more importantly, who is breeding the cats.

Many upstanding breeders would have the felines under their care tested and evaluated for any genetic conditions or diseases. And this is why it costs a little more to get a devon rex from a breeder than from other places, like a pet store or pet mill. Upstanding breeders would have the pets certified to be disease-free and cleared by a vet specialist. You will want to deal with a breeder who carries out these necessary health certifications at great lengths to screen and rule out genetic health problems and who will be willing to answer all your questions about the devon rex and its history.

Reputable breeders can be recognized easily because they too will have a few important questions to ask you. These are questions that will help them determine if the family and home the cat will be joining is a home who understands the responsibilities of taking care of a devon rex and is ready for it.

Finding a Reputable Devon Rex Breeder

The Internet is a good place to network with other devon rex owners and breeders. You will have to learn to recognize these sites and places to be able to trim down and sift out fly by night breeders from the good ones. You will need to learn to watch out for red flags that would give indication of things amiss with the people you will be talking to. The internet is a good place to start looking for devon rexs but be on the lookout for red flags such as the constant availability of kittens, the accessibility to credit card payments online.

These may sound convenient and standard procedure, but beware, because reputable breeders are almost never associated with these options or situations. Reputable breeders prefer to deal with potential cat guardians personally. They want to be able to impart information with and find out what a potential guardian has done in preparation for the new family addition.

Reputable breeders will also not have constant availability of kittens on wait. You shall have to go through the process of waiting. Breeders of good repute will add you on their waiting list most of the time. Devon Rexs are rare and there is a relatively small population of breeders who breed them. Check out breeders on this site <http://www.devonrexcats.com/devon-rex-breeders.html>

There is no sure-fire guarantee that the information here will help you better identify the intentions of a breeder. Nor does it assure you of the good or ill repute of the breeder you will choose to deal with, so asking the right questions is equally important when seeking out an honest and ethical breeder.

Some good questions you will want to ask any breeder you talk to is what sort of guarantee they give to kittens under their care. You will also want to ask what they would do if the kitten is later found to have a serious health condition. You will also want to discuss how the kitten was socialized; you will want to witness how the kittens interact and respond to the breeder. This will give you an idea of their personality and will assist in determining the amount of handling the litter of kittens has received.

Set expectations and be ready to wait for at least 6 months (sometimes more) for the right kitten to be made available. Since Russian Blues are a rare breed, Russian Blue breeders may not be easy to find nor is it around your vicinity. Use this time to do further research as you prepare and outfit your home for the eventual addition to your home.

Breeders of good standing will not release kittens to new homes until they are ready to be separated from its mother, or when it has weaned off the teat. This will mean you will have to wait another 12-16 weeks after their birth to have them join you. This time can be put to good use for you to make certain you have covered all bases and your home and its surroundings is ready for the new member to join the family ranks.

Selecting a Healthy Devon Rex

The funny-faced, pixie-looking Devon rex cats are known to be one of the most robust and healthiest felines in the cat spectrum. They enjoy an average lifespan of 10-15 years. This means many joyous years with your devon rex buddy. Because of proper care and attention, some of this cat sort has reported to live for as long as 20years! The devon rex is indeed a feline specie that enjoys quite a healthy life due to their resilience and fortunate circumstance of natural occurrence. And because they are a naturally occurring breed, this stroke of being blessed with good genes helps decrease and averts any likelihood of genetic abnormalities to plague them as other feline breeds are.

Make sure that you only deal with breeders who have carried out the proper screening tests for the cats before they are handed to you. Breeders of repute would have done the necessary initial tests and examinations and checkups for the cats before they close the deal.

Apart from the health guarantee you need to secure in paper from the breeder you will be dealing with, you too will have some silent observing to do. Request for a visit to the breeders facilities so that you can figure out and see for yourself the conditions in which the cats are housed. Ideally, a good breeder will allow you, not only access to their cat breeding and feline living facilities; they would also include you in the breeding process.

Selecting a healthy devon rex begins with the parents, the breeding pair. You will have to ask questions about their history and find out if they have gone through the proper medical screening examinations for HCM and other possible hereditary conditions. You will have to observe the demeanor and behavior of each of the mating cats. Are they mild or even tempered? Do they scare easy? Do they seem skittish and aloof? If they are then they may not be properly socialized and this trait may be passed on to the kittens.

Being able to see the breeding pair for yourself will allow you to see not only where the cats are housed, you will be able to observe how the cats interact with each other. When the new litter of kittens arrives, pay a visit and check out how the mother interacts with her new kittens. This time with the mother is important for the confidence and future well - being of the kittens. This time is vital for the proper socialization of the kittens later. Never accept a cat whose history is not determined, nor should you accept a kitten that is younger than 12 weeks. Good breeders will never release a cat earlier than that and opt to social the kitten with the mother for at least 12 - 16 weeks or when the kitten has been weaned off of the mother.

Although there are no guarantees that the kittens will not inherit any conditions the parents may have, there will be visual indications of the overall health of the kitten that you will be able to tell for yourself. The kittens should have clear eyes, clean ears, and smooth skin with no scars, scabs or bald spots. They should be able to walk and play. A kitten that has been removed from the rest of the litter is a bad indication.

Chapter Five: Housing and Safety of Your Devon Rex Cat

You will have to prepare your home and outfit it to welcome and integrate your new cat to your home. No matter what sort of pet a person decides to acquire, there will always be some sort of adjustments inside the home. You will have to take it upon yourself that the home you, your family and pets live in will be sound and safe for every member of your brood. Making sure that you have secured places where your kids and pets can interact and play will give you some peace of mind. It will also save you precious time with an otherwise unorganized, haphazard living condition.

Keeping Your Devon Rex Happy Indoors and Outdoors

Felines are well known to be endlessly and utterly curious little beasts. Reference to their mischief, penchant in getting itself in precarious situations and playfulness has been recorded many times over quotes and sayings. There are so many of these sayings that give sufficient evidence to this claim. Your devon rex is typically classified as a moderately active cat. Meaning, they will do what cats will do, and then some! Your furry buddy from the shores across the pond is a playful little beast that will want to be in your business all the time.

They will hound your very steps around the house and meticulously inspect the chore you are busy with, checking to see if it is up to par, or how they may "help". They will be there to chime in and give their two cents worth about the job you are doing. So it is absolutely imperative that you are able to outfit your home in a way that your cats are engaged with the right sort of activity any given time you won't be available for some downtime with them.

Devon rex cats are not only robust little things, they are also eager eaters and will try to get their little paws on food when it is made available. Therefore you will want to set rules and boundaries, or you will have to keep chasing away your devon rex from consuming meant-for-human foods you set out. Aside from these mentioned, there are a few other things around and about the house you will have to consider which we have listed below.

- Take stock of the foliage around your home. Ever notice cats busily munch on plants? Well, they will. Therefore it is important that you get to know the sort of plants that are growing in your planter, yard, or land. It is important that the cat is kept from roaming in areas where you have not been able to identify the plant. There is a host of toxic plants that are toxic to felines which can cause the cat's demise. Even non-poisonous plants can cause vomiting and diarrhea in a cat and you don't want to risk sudden illness. You may want to consider replanting plants or better yet, replace the plants with ones that are safe for cats.

- The devon rex is lauded as one of the most intelligent of cat breeds and can be trained to do some play tricks, making them really engaging house mates. Throw them a ball, and watch them fetch it for you. Call out their name often enough, they will understand that it is them you are addressing and may even respond. They are so smart that they can even pick up habits and actions their human wards. Make it a point that your doors are fitted with safety latches that would difficult for your cat to paw open. All you need to do is give your devon rex a little time to get to know it, and you will discover the keen sensibilities of this feline.

- Lock away all medicine, vitamins, supplements, ointments, pills and creams. Your devon rex is an inquisitive little guy who will want to investigate these objects. There is a host of human medicine which can pose great danger to any pet if they get to them and ingest these. Minimize the risk of this happening by storing away any and all sorts of medication.

- If you have favorite baubles and trinkets adorning your home, you may want to rethink their places in the home. Cats are fantastic explorers who have a great need to satisfy their curious nature. You will definitely want to limit the access of your cats to some rooms or store your favorite knick knacks away from the general areas where they are allowed. Outfit the family room with scratching posts so that they do not scratch up your furniture. It is best to rub a little catnip on the pot so they gravitate to this item when they get the urge to trim their nails. Set out litter boxes in areas away from the general activity area, so as the cats are comfortable to do natures business in peace.

- Make it a habit to pull out electric cords from unused sockets. Cats have an attraction to anything that mimics string. You wouldn't want the cat to suffer from an accidental shock should it start chewing on a live wire. Get some of those commercially produced wire guards to help protect your electronic cords, and your cat, from damage and injury.

- Curtain ropes and blind strings are other things in the home which the cat will take fancy. Make it a point to keep blind cords and drapery ropes coiled and out of your cats reach. Your playful cat may just find itself in a dangerous situation by getting itself tangled up on rope. Reduce the possibility of accidents by removing anything the cat may mistake for toys.

- You playful devon rex s not unlike most cats. Most cats enjoy lounging in dark, cool, and tight spaces. There are more than a ton of video collections that attests to this natural aversion of the feline. Make sure that you secure doors and windows where they can get access to the outside world. Make sure that you check the interior tubs of washers and dryers before throwing in the clothes. Make sure that the doors of any household machinery are kept shut at all times.

- Another place cats like to hang out is under cars. So make sure you honk your horn before pulling out of the driveway. Aside for possible larger-animal attacks, this reason is another strong argument as to why cats are better kept indoors.

- Setting out a nice table for invited guests? Make sure your devon rex does not get wind of the event or they will want to come as well. Table cloths are great curiosities for felines as drapes are. Make sure that you do not leave your cat in places where they may disrupt your dinner placement arrangements. Save your best china from multiplying in shards, and your cat a tongue-lashing.

- Keep toilet lids closed and make sure that you set out fresh bowls of water for your cats. Do not risk your curious devon rex kitten from falling into the bowl unattended. This is important to remember most especially if the cat will be left alone for most of the day.

- You will soon discover the jumping, leaping and climbing dexterity of your devon rex. If you have more than one growing devon rex living with you, you will want to train it to not jump up on your kitchen counter or anywhere around the sink. Since they will be investigative snoopers who are able to to learn easy, repeated actions it sees you do. Cover garbage disposal switches lest your cats manage to work their way around flicking it on.

- Once more, you want to keep your Russian Blue indoors as an indoor cat - this measure of security will ward off would-be cat - nappers from carting your RB away. You will want to make sure that your door and window screens do not have tears from which they can exit. You will want to have securely fastened screens and sturdy latches to lessen the risk of your feline slipping out of the safety of its home unnoticed.

- Conduct a quick check on all screens of doors and windows. Make sure there are no tears or holes from which the cat may escape.

- Keep all uneaten food covered and tucked where the cat won't be able to reach. The devon rex has a large appetite and you will soon discover this when they complain and ask for more food - even after you've fed them!

Toys and Accessories

Your devon rex will be spending most of its life indoors, save from the occasional supervised forays you take it on. Make sure that you have the proper equipment, tools, sundries and toys. Your devon rex is a relatively independent cat, but absolutely needs quality time with you. If you are a person who is at home most times of the day, you will find the devon rex to be a great companion. Should you be the sort who will need to leave your cats alone for an extended period, you will want to invest in a few mechanical toys that will keep your cats engaged whilst you are away.

Visit nearby pet shops around you and the ones online to check out some of the more innovative inventions to keep your cats engaged and entertained during their alone time at home. Some of these toys not only engage them mentally and physically, some of these actually give reward treats to the cat. Attach bells and chimes they can reach from a low level. Putting these shiny, tinkling toys at cat eye-level will give them hours and hours of fun by themselves or as your cats take turns. There are also puzzle and reward machines that you will be able to find in the market.

Other devices not only stimulate the cat to think about how to get the reward, it also makes the cat "work" for the treat, thereby stimulating not only the mind but the physical abilities and dexterity of your devon rex. A laser-light pointer to chase after and follow is an inexpensive toy that you can get in random places, but there should be some available at pet shops. This can create lots of fun for you and your cat as well as some much needed exercise for your cat. You will definitely want to grab a feather or ribbon teaser which is another great exercise aid for your cats. Soft balls and squeaky toys are still an all - time hit for felines, so put out a few of these around the allowed areas.

Chapter Six: Feeding and Nutrition of Your Devon Rex Cat

As with people and other pets, RBC will thrive best and be at its healthiest with the proper nutrition. So choosing the proper foods that will meet its nutritional requirements is a must. Remember that the RBC is one of the feline breeds least likely to be prone to feline illnesses, so you will be able to rest easier knowing that caring for it will not be as complicated. Choosing the right foods to feed your new RB cat will be crucial to its continued good health. Today, feline guardians have a world of choices when choosing what sort of foods to feed their pets. Empower yourself and study up on what ingredients manufacturers use to produce their pet food.

Learn to read labels and decipher complicated-sounding ingredients. Know the jargons and wordings manufacturers use to market their products. Do your research and ask reputable breeders for recommendations they may be able to offer. Talk to your pet's health provider about your RBs diet and have the vet determine which kind of food will best work to your cat's advantage.

Feeding Your Devon: From Kitten to Maturity

The diet of a devon rex cat is not a demanding one. It does it require any one thing in specific to its diet. They have no unusual needs when it comes to getting them the proper nutrition. Devon rexs are known to be hearty eaters who are not picky about the type of cat food served up to them. They are typically satisfied with any sort of cat food and will usually demand a second helping. Food is definitely on top of a devon rexs priority list, closely followed by its desire and need for your love and attention.

Beware the food you have prepared and laid out for the family, because they are stealthy little critters who will always be happy to have another serving. Even after a good hardy feeding, devon rexs are masters at convincing you that they haven't been fed enough and will beg you for more. Do not give in and make sure that you put away food meant for the family away until it is time for meals. Not only will they try to get more food from the table, your devon rex cat will also try to get away with asking for more. Giving in to its imploring mews and begging eyes would encourage in it a bad habit of overeating. This can lead to obesity and a less active lifestyle for the usually active and playful devon rex.

Overeating causes obesity and cats suffering from this become prone to bone and joint problems caused by the heaviness of the excess weight its tiny frame has to carry. This condition can be exorbitantly exaggerated by the feline preferring to lead a stoic and stagnant lifestyle, not wanting to move, play, jump about or exercise.

The recommended feeding frequency for a devon rex kitten is three separate feedings throughout the day until the kitten reaches 7 months old. Once it is past the 7 month milestone, lessen the feeding frequency of your devon rex to two times a day. Seasoned caregivers and experts of the devon rex cat suggest feeding the cat a premium dry cat food that is grain free. Grain free foods mean the product has less "fillers" in the mixture. This ensures that only usable nutrients are present in the meals. Grain free, premium dry cat food may seem a tad more expensive than most grocery store brands, however, this in fact makes for less additional supplements with this kind of food and your cat gets to benefit health wise in the long run while you enjoy a bit of long term savings. Another benefit to premium dry cat food is there will be fewer poops to scoop out of your feline's litter box.

Essential Nutrients

The overall good health of the devon rex will save you, their favorite human ward, from spending for costly an unexpected health care as long as you do your bit in taking care of it in the proper manner it deserves and needs. This stroke of good health leaves you with a greater budget to serve up top quality, tasty food for your loyal devon rex.

The correct provision of optimum dry pet food will essentially provide all the nutritional needs of the devon rex. Learn to choose the correct sorts of foods, because you will want to give your devon rex a variety of health and nutrition laden food, which will provide them the right dietary measures they need. Providing them with the right sort of high quality pet food will supply your feline all the vitamins, minerals and nutrients it would need to thrive and enjoy good health.

As time passes and your devon rex matures you will have to lessen meal frequency from three times a day to two meals each day, and possibly adding more food to each of the two servings.

Chapter Seven: The Kinds of Foods and Ingredients to Avoid

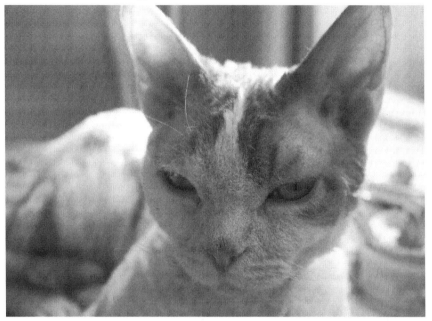

There are many pet food manufacturers that label their food with tags like "meals" and "by-products", stay away from them. These pet foods are made out of questionable animal parts that were not used in the processing of foods meant for humans. These meat parts could come from any unusable parts of a cow, pork, or chicken. These meat parts are leftovers from processing human food and can be any animal part from chicken feet, beak, or legs, tongue, nose, paws, tail, or ear, and the list goes on.

A host of additives are mixed in to mask the inferiority of the food product. You need to remember that lots of preservatives are carcinogens to humans and causes cancer. When preservatives are used to make pet food these ingredients limit bacteria growth and inhibit food oxidation. Remember that choosing the right sort of healthy food for your pet will largely fall on your shoulders. Your pet will not mind how the food you serve appears, only how the food would taste.

To raise a healthier devon rex you will want to stay away from pet food products that contain preservatives like BHT, BHA, sodium nitrate, and nitrate. Pet manufacturers who use artificial coloring use them to make the food more attractive to the look. Bear in mind that these have no important or impactful nutritional value and the effects of these ingredients may pose later health risks and allergic reactions.

Types of Commercial Cat Foods

Premium dry cat food is one of the best choices in food variants for your feline pet and will come highly recommended. Premium dry foods have a longer shelf life, and it also helps clean the teeth of your feline. The optimum kind will provide your feline the proper and overall nourishment of your fluffy buddy.

Premium grade canned food, mixed in with a bit of water, is another food choice for your cats which will sufficiently sustain your devon rexs nutritional requirements. Canned pet food does not last as long outside the can as dry cat food would and food from the can will need to be consumed within a short period of time after it has been set out. However, premium grade canned food will provide the proper overall nutrients your feline needs.

Talk to your vet about alternative ways to feed your devon rex kittens and cats. Should you decide to feed it home - cooked meals ask for a diet plan suitable for the cat. Home -cooked meals may take more time to gather and prepare. Home - cooked foods and its sound nutritional components is largely determined by the quality of the freshness of the ingredients used. Remember that you will need to measure out specific portions of the ingredients in correct amounts to get the proper nutritional balance for your feline buddy.

Fresh Water

Cats are known to be timid water drinkers and often times need to be reminded to take a sip of water. Water is a very important component that helps the cat cool down and hydrate itself. Make certain that fresh water is always set out for your cats to drink from at any given time of the day.

It has been observed that cats would favor drinking running water from a fountain to drinking still water from a bowl. Whichever choice they take to, you should always leave out a fresh bowl of water for your devon rex to drink from at all times.

Food Additives

The inclusion of food additives in any pet food product is to be questioned by any potential devon rex owner. As a new pet owner, you will need to develop uncanny skills of deciphering food labels in order to confidently serve up only the most nutritious food to your devon rex. Some of these food additives are utilized to enhance the quality and safety of the food then there are those which are utterly unhealthy and only added to use as fillers and extenders, giving the food added volume and luster.

Tips for Selecting a High-Quality Cat Food Brand

You will need to be in the know in order to not be swayed by commercial food hype. You will have to take it upon yourself to learn to read and decipher labels. You will need to take it upon yourself to understand what sort of ingredients go into the pet food you get for your pets.

Most high-end, expensive brands will talk about the high quality ingredients used in their products. It will be up to you to find that out by learning to read the labels of the products you buy for your felines. Products labeled as gourmet or premium are not bound to include better quality ingredients in the food they manufacture, than other less costly, balanced and complete pet foods.

Foods that are labeled "Natural" contain components derived only from animal, plant or mined resources. Natural foods are foods that cannot be overly processed. These foods should not contain synthetic ingredients like preservatives, artificial flavors, or coloring. There are different levels of organic food. Whatever percentage a labels boasts is the percentage of organic ingredients used in the production of the food.

Organic pet foods are food ingredients that did not use artificial fertilizers or conventional pesticides when these were being grown. These pet food components are free of contamination from human or industrial wastes. These foods are not processed through ionizing radiation. Nor do they add food additives to the food. If animal meats are involved in the production of the pet foods, the animals would have been raised without the use of antibiotics or growth hormones. These near-organically raised animals would have been fed a healthy diet.

How (Much) To Feed Your Devon Rex

There will be a period of experimenting on the sort of food your devon rex will take a liking to at the beginning. Take time to learn how to read labels and be a food detective for the health and wellbeing of your devon rex. Purchase small quantities of various pet food products. It will be easy to tell which foods they prefer and which ones they don't. Make sure that you get to know which foods they prefer. Devon rexes are hardy eaters so, a devon rex minus the hearty appetite may be ill or at the very least, dislikes the fare set out before them; being an observant human will work for the best advantage of all.

In order to avoid food wastage and spoilage, you will need to experiment with the amount of food you give to your cat at the onset. To know how much food you need to give your devon rex for each meal, set out two cups of premium dry cat food in a slow-feeding bowl. The dish is to be offered to the cat for the next 30 minutes and should be eaten out of within that given time. Once done eating, measure the remaining dry food left in the feeding bowl. Subtract the leftovers from the initial 2 cups of food you set out for your cat and you will come up with the amount of food your devon rex is capable of eating each meal. The "missing" amount of food would be the proper quantity to leave out for your cat for its succeeding meals.

This procedure may have to be repeated for the next 2-3 days to get an accurate measurement of the amount of food intake your kitten is able to consume. Start reducing the frequency of feeding when your devon rex reaches its 7th month. An older devon rex cat will not have to eat as often as a growing kitten would, however, it will be necessary to add more food to each meal when feeding frequency is tapered. Pay attention to the food you set out for the more mature kitten to avoid over feeding, food spoilage and wastage.

Chapter Eight: Guidelines in Caring For Your Devon Rex Cat

By now you have come to understand how easy it is to care for and live with a devon rex. It thrives well with frequent contact with its humans and loves the attention you give them. They are good eaters with healthy appetites and are generally healthy cats due to their natural occurrence. There are however some breeders who have been experimenting with the devon rex genes to come up with different colored cats that are unusual of the natural occurring cats.

Overall, it is important to deal with a reputable breeder who will be upfront about the pros and cons of the devon rex in question. This next chapter will talk about other important things vital to your successful union with a devon rex.

Socializing Your Devon Rex Cat

Once integrated into the family and when the devon rex has made strong ties within the cat will be soon be in tune with the emotions its human's experiences. Devon rexs are known to be very sympathetic felines. They are able to detect, and identify with, the emotions of their humans and you will notice it try to gently engage you when it knows you are in a funk. The sweet devon rex will try to cheer you up on days when you seem to be stuck under a grey cloud.

Devon rexs, with other devon rexs for company, can fare well on their own when you have to be at work. Having another devon rex, or another friendly pet they can interact with, to keep them company would be the best environment for these elfish-looking cats. They tend to make better friends with those who share similar traits as they possess. But it will require your attention and seek your company when you are at home. To reject its advances and refuse it time and attention may hurt your furry friend's feelings.

Repeated and constant rejection may cause the cat to develop anxiety and feelings of insecurity. Therefore, allot ample time to catch up with your devon rexs when you get home. It will be hard not to anyway.

Initially, the devon rex may show trepidation and weariness with its new surroundings. This is natural for anyone being introduced to a new environment. They will soon enough get used to the new place and you will see how easily it will adapt to the new home it has been welcomed. Once it becomes familiar with its surroundings the devon rex will gravitate toward the human members of their brood who it deems worthy of their attention. It will be friendly not only to the people of the family but even friends of the family who they often see in the mix.

Training Your Devon Rex

Training your Devon Rex during the early stages of kitten hood will give the kitten the advantage of growing up well-mannered and well-rounded. Teaching your young devon rex will reap the best results when they are started out as a young kitten. They are one of the smartest feline breeds and are often likened to dogs or monkeys in their level of ability to learn. They are quick to get tricks and are also able to recognize command words. It is imperative to maintain a high level of discipline during the training period.

It is important to know that the devon rex, with its high level of intelligence, will seem to "own" you more than the other way around. The devon rex will actually think that you are their pet and would attempt to do the directing of events around the home. If you do not want to be overpowered by your little fur balls, make sure that you put your foot down and let them know who gives the orders around the house.

Effective training will require instant reward or immediate punishment after an action. Putting off reward or punishment 5-10 minutes later defeats the purpose of training because the cat will not understand what merited its reward or punishment if not given immediately.

It isn't rare to hear stories of devon rexs learning to open doors or lids, so you will want to be selective about what your devon rex learns. It is also not unusual to hear about devon rexs learning to switch machinery on and off, and this can be dangerous especially if you are out of the house for extended periods of time. Your keen attention and consistency in handing out reward and punishment is vital to it learning.

Network with other seasoned devon rex owners on internet sites and ask your vet for tips and recommendations on how to train your cat. They would also be able to tell you where to look for pet trainers for your new curly-furred devon rex. Finding and working with a good cat trainer is an option available to you should you not have the time, patience or ability to train them on your own. You will still need to make sure to make time for this important milestone your devon rex. You will after all, be the one the cat will be getting its commands from, so your presence is still important during training sessions with a trainer.

Behaviour of the Devon Rex

Devon Rex cats are highly intelligent felines and have been observed to be very trainable. The cat owner should express keen attention and consistency. These are key factors to successfully correcting any behavioral problems the cat may display.

A human caregiver has to be consistent in responding the same manner each time an undesirable action is carried out by the cat. If your devon rex cat does something beyond the bounds of the rules you have set, like taking food from the dinner table, you will need to consistently address this issue the same manner each time it happens until the cat understands the action to be unacceptable and that you will not tolerate this behavior.

Calling out your cat's name loudly followed by command words like "No!" or "Down!" and loudly clapping your hands should deter your cat from further mischief. You can also use a spray bottle which you would spray its way when an unacceptable action is carried out by your feline. This is why the first few weeks of supervision during integration of cat and human is important. Make it a point to be there or have someone who will also be responsible for the care of the cat to be present.

Be consistent about calling out your new pet for any undesirable actions and ill behaviors. Be sure to reinforce the lesson each time with harmless but disciplinary measures that they remember, understand and recognize- such as aiming a spray of water its way and by loud clapping your hands as you sternly call out your cat's name.

Devon Rexs love the interaction they have with you and could become anxious or fearful when it doesn't get the equal amount of affection it gives you. Your devon rex is a one feline specie who does not appreciate being ignored. It could feel hurt when the affection it gives is not returned. It will be important that you reciprocate their love and factor in spending quality time with your devon rex.

Take time to play and catch up with your little devon rex at least 10 to 15 minutes, twice each day. The more time you spend with it, the happier it will be.

Chapter Nine: Grooming Your Devon Rex

The devon rex is really one of the cat species which requires minimal maintenance. It is one of the cleanest cats you will ever get to know and you will learn this through their habits of keeping itself clean. The devon rex, like most other cat sorts, is also very finicky about toilet hygiene. As their human guardian, you will have to be consistent about keeping its toilet space spotless by clearing out their litter boxes at least twice a day. The devon rex is thought to be a low-maintenance feline in terms of grooming needs. Aside from the monthly routine of giving them an occasional bath, you will only need to clean out their ears once a week and check that their nails are not growing out of proportion that it would cause pain or injury.

Required grooming of a devon rex is minimal but necessary. An occasional comb run over its coat, and periodical nail clipping is really all a devon rex needs. Down time can also be a good time to inspect your devon rex for any bald spots on its body. Routinely checking up the cat's physique will allow you to determine if the cat has fleas and ticks.

Nail Trimming

Occasional nail trimming is advisable in order to avert the cat's natural tendency to sharpen its claws on furniture you have around the house. You want to start introducing this grooming procedure while the devon rex is young so it grows up used to periodic maintenance as it matures.

You should have the first trimming done at a grooming shop or at your vet's clinic. Observe how they do this and learn before you attempt to do this on your own. Finding a nail trimming tool may need some experimentation on your end. When you figure out which tool the cat responds to with the least resistance, you should invest on a similar implement to use for grooming when at home.

Keep in mind that you will always have to cut above the pink of the nail. Cutting too far in could cause injury to the cat as well as profuse bleeding from nicks when cut too far into the nail.

Your devon rex is an intelligent little feline who you will discover to be highly trainable. Exposing it to regular grooming activities early in its life will teach it be more accepting of these routinary grooming procedures as it matures. The earlier a feline is exposed to some forms of routine, the higher the likelihood of it showing acceptance and agreeability.

Tooth Brushing

No one likes morning breath on anyone, so introduce dental hygiene while your devon rex is young so that it grows up used to this other necessary grooming procedure. Your devon rex cat will need a good mouth cleaning at least four times a month at minimum. This will help it keep a healthy head of teeth and avoid periodontal diseases.

Introduce teeth cleaning while the kitten young and continue with this mouth cleaning routine on a scheduled basis. Purchase a toothbrush that will comfortably fit the cat's mouth. Make sure that you use toothpaste meant for pets. Using human toothpaste on your devon rex is a great no-no because these may contain dangerous or toxic ingredients which can affect felines negatively.

Bathing

It is generally unnecessary but you may bathe your devon rex should it become too dirty for itself to clean on their own. You may give them a monthly bath in a tub of warm water and use cleaning agents meant for cats.

Chapter Ten: Breeding and Showing Your Devon Rex

The devon rex is indeed a great cat to have around the house because of its unique traits and loyalty. It is also a joy to show off to friends and family. It is no wonder that owners of devon rexs have the strong desire to share their cat's goofy, intelligent antics to the rest of the world of cat fanciers. If you are looking to do the same, find out what it would take to get your devon rex cat in the show ring.

Devon Rex Breed Standard- Cat Fanciers Association

HEAD (40)
- shape and size - 12
- muzzle - 5
- profile and chin - 6
- eyes - 5
- ears - 12

BODY (25)
- trunk and tail - 10
- paws and legs - 10
- neck - 5

COAT (30)
- thickness - 10
- texture and length - 10
- wave of the coat - 10

COLOUR (5)

GENERAL: A feline of a good show specimen should be in optimum physical condition, its muscle tone should be firm, and it must be alert.

The Devon Rex with its big eyes, short muzzle, pronounced cheekbones, and massive, low set ears make up their characteristic elfin appearance. It is a feline with a medium fine frame, and is properly coated in soft, wavy fur. Its coat has a distinct feel due to the mutation which gives it a wavy coat. It is an active cat that is alert and shows great interest in its environment.

HEAD: A show grade devon rex feline's head is show a modified wedge. When viewed from the front the wedge of the head is marked with a narrowing series of 3 pronounced convex curves. The head is to show broad and slightly longer. Its face is to be full-cheeked with its cheekbones prominent with whisker breaks. When viewed from the side, its nose is to display a pronounced stop, with its forehead curving back to the flat of its cranium. Stud jowls in adult males are given allowance.

MUZZLE: The optimal show devon rex's muzzle should be a short and well-developed with prominent whisker pads apparent.

CHIN: The chin of a show grade devon rex should be well-developed and strong. When viewed from the side, the chin has to align vertically with its nose. Neither overshot nor undershot.

EARS: The show feline's ears should be strikingly massive and set low on the sides of its head. The outside base of the ears should extend beyond the wedge point of the head. Its ears should taper off to rounded tips and covered completely with fine fur.

EYES: The eyes of a show quality devon rex is to be large set wide apart. The eyes of the devon rex should be oval in shape and must slope on the outer edges of its ears. Any eye color is acceptable.

NECK: Its neck should be medium long and slender.

NOSE: Its nose should be medium in length.

BODY: The body of the show feline should be lithe, firm, of medium length, hard as it is muscular. It should be broad in the chest area and medium fine in boning. Its legs are also to be medium fine in boning as they are sturdy. The body is to be carried high on the legs. The hind legs of the show devon rex is to be longer than those of the front. As long as proportions are maintained, allowance for the larger sized male devon rex is given.

LEGS: The hind legs of the feline are to be long, medium fine boned and longer than the forelegs of the cat.

PAWS: The paws of the cat are to be small and slightly oval. Its toes are to be counted five on each front paw and should count four on each hind leg.

TAIL: Its tail should be long and fine. It should taper and must be completely covered with short fur.

COAT: The coat of the show quality devon rex is to cover its whole body. The thickest part of the coat should be apparent on the back area of the cat, as its sides, legs, tail, ears and face. Less density is allowed on the neck, chest, abdomen and top of the head. Serious faults are called when bare patches are apparent in an adult devon rex, and a fault when seen in kittens. Down on the undersides of the devon rex's body is not to be interpreted as bareness. The scarcity of fur on the forehead in front of the ears is not considered as a fault.

TEXTURE: The coat of the devon rex is fine, full-bodied, rexed and soft to the touch.

PENALIZE: Heads that are shown too long and/or too narrow, as well as heads that taper in a V fashion, craniums with ears that are flared, heads showing to be too round rather than tapered, or any hint of a mixed breed, are to be faulted and penalized. An extremely short muzzle is also to be penalized, as with a bite that is misaligned, ears that are small or set too high up the head is also a penalty. A bare tail or a short one also merits penalty. A straight coat or bare patches on the fur are also penalized.

DISQUALIFY: An immediate disqualification is called for when a devon rex is shown to have excessive baldness. It is disqualified if it has a shaggy coat or fur that is excessively long. Disqualification is deemed for a devon rex who has long hair on the tail area, or if its tail is abnormal or kinked. It is also disqualified for not having the proper number of toes, or for weak hind legs. A devon rex is disqualified if its eyes show to have defect or is cross eyed. Any sign or indications of weakness or ill health merits disqualification.

DEVON REX COLOURS

COLOUR: Allowable colors and patterns come in any of the genetically possible outcomes as well as any combination of genetically possible patterns.

Breeding Your Devon Rex - Cfa Individual Registration

The application to register your pet with the Cat Fanciers Association will have to be supplied and applied for by the breeder. Get in touch with and talk to the breeder who you got your devon rex from and ask for the

Application for Registry which is also referred to as a "blue slip".

A common practice for reputable breeders of pedigree cats is to withhold the release of the blue slip, and have certain conditions to be met before they do. A reputable breeder could choose to withhold the release of the blue slip especially if your purchase agreement states that the cat has first to be spayed or neutered before the registration documents are handed over to you.

If this agreement is not satisfied, there is nothing the CFA can do until these contract terms are satisfied. For the CFA to give registration to an individual feline in the absence of the standard application form, you will have to provide supporting documents along with a request letter to the CFA.

The documents you will need to provide would be a pedigree or another supporting document, provided for by the breeder, establishing the eligibility of the feline to be registered under the Cat Fanciers Association. Information from this would include the date of birth of the pet to be registered along with the parent's CFA registration numbers. Other information to be furnished is proof that the cat was bought with or without breeding rights.

An owner of a devon rex could also provide a copy of the written purchase agreement clearly stating the terms and conditions of the acquisition. This document must be signed by all concerned parties, indicating that CFA papers are to be provided. The birth date and identifying CFA registration numbers of the parents of the pet being registered must also be provided whether the feline was bought with or without the right to breed.

Other acceptable documentation to support your application would be copies of all canceled cheques as well as receipts providing proof of full payment. Copies of other documents indicating compliance of all other prerequisites to the release of the application form, provided by the breeder may also be required. When these documents are received, the Central Office will call the breeder and request their cooperation and/or comments to speed up resolution.

In the event of incomplete document or information submission, the Central Office will not be able to give you any assistance until such time of document completion and submission.

You will want to clarify each detail of the agreement with the breeder. Figure out early on, if you want your female devon rex to mate and breed later on. Determining these details at an early stage of the acquisition will allow you to set expectations with your breeder. Have all appropriate requirements transfer hands and documentation of all minor dealings (receipt, certifications, record of screening tests, etc.) filed away and ready at a moment's notice.

What to Know When Planning To Breed Your Devon Rex

So you want to breed your devon rex. This is a detail you want to determine early on if you intend to register your cat with the CFA. For the CFA to register a devon rex feline with breeding privileges a PIN written on the blue slip has to be provided by the devon rex breeder.

This PIN combination is to be written inside the PIN box of the Application for Registration or the blue slip. This PIN combination is a 5-digit, randomly generated number which will be reflected only on the Certificate of Litter Registration given to the breeder.

Each litter registered will be given a different PIN and will be assigned solely to that particular litter. Only the breeder of the litter to be registered will have access to this PIN. The CFA will have no record of this PIN.

In the instance of a change of heart and mind and the cat was previously registered with the CFA as a Not For Breeding Cat, get in touch with the devon rex breeder to get the Litter PIN. Write down the PIN on the registration certificate and bring it to the CFA with specific request to change the present NFB registration to that of a breeding cat. There is a $15.00 fee to pay for this modification.

Care Sheet and Summary

This chapter will give you a quick summary of all the important things you need to take note in keeping a Devon Rex cat. Once you've acquired this breed, it's now up to you to apply all the things you've learned in this book. It's also wise that you keep learning by attending cat shows, and talking to other Devon Rex keepers or breeders. This way you can gain more insights and tips on how you can better take care of your new pet. We hope that you become a responsible breeder! Good luck!

A Summary of Facts about the Devon Rex Cat

- **Pedigreed:** by the Cat Fanciers' Association, TICA, and AACE
- **Breed Size:** Medium
- **Height:** 10 - 12 inches (25 - 35 cm) tall
- **Weight:** 8 - 10 lbs. for both male and females
- **Coat Texture:** wild curly soft suede - like
- **Color:** white, black, blue, chocolate, cinnamon, lavender and red
- **Coat Pattern:** smoke patterns in its white undercoat
- **Eyes:** The eyes of the devon rex should be oval in shape and must slope on the outer edges of its ears. Any eye color is acceptable.
- **Ears:** The show feline's ears should be strikingly massive and set low on the sides of its head.
- **Nose:** Its nose should be medium in length.
- **Body:** The body of the show feline should be lithe, firm, of medium length, hard as it is muscular.
- **Legs:** The hind legs of the feline are to be long, medium fine boned
- **Tail:** Its tail should be long and fine.

- **Temperament:** The devon rex is such an intelligent cat that it has been given many monikers. Since it has a personality and extends loyalty much like a canine would it has been likened to a dog. Devon Rex cats share particular genetic traits but you will find the joy of getting to know each devon rex and discover how, much like people, diverse they are in moods and personality.

- **Socializing:** Devon rexs, with other devon rexs for company, can fare well on their own when you have to be at work. Having another devon rex, or another friendly pet they can interact with, to keep them company would be the best environment for these elfish-looking cats. They tend to make better friends with those who share similar traits as they possess.

- **Devon Rex Cats with other pets:** Anyone considering one devon rex would fare better if they decided to bring home two of this beautiful breed. Not only do they enjoy your loving and attentive companionship, they also love being around and playing with other pets, no matter what animal they may be. Being raised with another devon rex will be conducive to the cats mental and physical health. Not only would they have the companionship they would need for times when you are out at work.

- **Training:** Highly trainable and adapts easily to people who handle them gently.

- **Playtime Needs:** frequent, active playtime exercise is encouraged strongly.

- **Health Conditions:**

  o Hypertrophic cardiomyopathy (HCM) is a typical form of heart disease seen in cats. This heart disease causes hypertrophy, a thickening of the heart muscle. A vet would be able to confirm this by ordering an echocardiogram which can confirm if a feline has HCM. You will want to cross out breeders from your lists who claim to have HCM-free kittens in their breed. No one can give any sort of guarantee that the felines under their care will never develop the condition

  o A hereditary problem which may require surgical correction is patellar luxation. This genetically passed on condition involves the popping out of the cat's kneecap. This condition would cause the cat to limp or hop when in movement.

- **Grooming needs:** Required grooming of a devon rex is minimal but necessary. An occasional comb run over its coat, and periodical nail clipping is really all a devon rex needs. Down time can also be a good time to inspect your devon rex for any bald spots on its body. Routinely checking up the cat's physique will allow you to determine if the cat has fleas and ticks.

- **Lifespan:** typical average lifespan is 10 - 15 years

Basic Nutritional Information

- **Nutritional Needs:** diet rich in meats (chicken or beef), grains, oats, egg yolks, protein, calcium from cream cheese, yogurt, buttermilk, iron from liver.

- **Water Consumption:** frequent replenishment of water dish is advised.

- **Feeding Amount:** varies on specific factors like history, gender, weight, size, age.

- **Feeding Frequency:** It is best to consult with your vet about the amount of food you put out for your cat.

- **Mixed Foods**: include allowed veggies like carrots, broccoli into meals.

- **Grains**: include grains and oats in its diet.

Cat Accessories and Expenses

- Bed and blankets: $25 - $75
- Kitten Food: $15-$30
- Treats: $5 - $15
- Feeders and bowls: $50 - $150
- Collar, Harness and/or Leash: $5 - $20
- Brush: $4 - $50
- Trimmers and Clippers: $6 - $50
- Litter: $5 - $35
- Litter Boxes: $15 - $200
- Waste Disposal: $3 - $30
- Filters and deodorants: $4 - $25
- Liners and mats: $2 - $40
- Toys: $1 - $50
- Toy Crate: $10 - $150
- Cat carrier: $25 - $200
- Vaccination for kittens: $50 - $100
- Vet visit: $35 - $50
- Kitten Food: $15-$30

- Treats: $5 - $15
- Litter: $5 - $35
- Waste Disposal: $3 - $30
- Filters and deodorants: $4 - $25
- Liners and mats: $2 - $40

Glossary of Cat Terms

Abundism – Referring to a cat that has markings more prolific than is normal.

Acariasis – A type of mite infection.

ACF – Australian Cat Federation

Affix – A cattery name that follows the cat's registered name; cattery owner, not the breeder of the cat.

Agouti – A type of natural coloring pattern in which individual hairs have bands of light and dark coloring.

Ailurophile – A person who loves cats.

Albino – A type of genetic mutation which results in little to no pigmentation, in the eyes, skin, and coat.

Allbreed – Referring to a show that accepts all breeds or a judge who is qualified to judge all breeds.

Alley Cat – A non-pedigreed cat.

Alter – A desexed cat; a male cat that has been neutered or a female that has been spayed.

Amino Acid – The building blocks of protein; there are 22 types for cats, 11 of which can be synthesized and 11 which must come from the diet (see essential amino acid).

Anestrus – The period between estrus cycles in a female cat.

Any Other Variety (AOV) – A registered cat that doesn't conform to the breed standard.

ASH – American Shorthair, a breed of cat.

Back Cross – A type of breeding in which the offspring is mated back to the parent.

Balance – Referring to the cat's structure; proportional in accordance with the breed standard.

Barring – Describing the tabby's striped markings.

Base Color – The color of the coat.

Bicolor – A cat with patched color and white.

Blaze – A white coloring on the face, usually in the shape of an inverted V.

Bloodline – The pedigree of the cat.

Brindle – A type of coloring, a brownish or tawny coat with streaks of another color.

Castration – The surgical removal of a male cat's testicles.

Cat Show – An event where cats are shown and judged.

Cattery – A registered cat breeder; also, a place where cats may be boarded.

CFA – The Cat Fanciers Association.

Cobby – A compact body type.

Colony – A group of cats living wild outside.

Color Point – A type of coat pattern that is controlled by color point alleles; pigmentation on the tail, legs, face, and ears with an ivory or white coat.

Colostrum – The first milk produced by a lactating female; contains vital nutrients and antibodies.

Conformation – The degree to which a pedigreed cat adheres to the breed standard.

Cross Breed – The offspring produced by mating two distinct breeds.

Dam – The female parent.

Declawing – The surgical removal of the cat's claw and first toe joint.

Developed Breed – A breed that was developed through selective breeding and crossing with established breeds.

Down Hairs – The short, fine hairs closest to the body which keep the cat warm.

DSH – Domestic Shorthair.

Estrus – The reproductive cycle in female cats during which she becomes fertile and receptive to mating.

Fading Kitten Syndrome – Kittens that die within the first two weeks after birth; the cause is generally unknown.

Feral – A wild, untamed cat of domestic descent.

Gestation – Pregnancy; the period during which the fetuses develop in the female's uterus.

Guard Hairs – Coarse, outer hairs on the coat.

Harlequin – A type of coloring in which there are van markings of any color with the addition of small patches of the same color on the legs and body.

Inbreeding – The breeding of related cats within a closed group or breed.

Kibble – Another name for dry cat food.

Lilac – A type of coat color that is pale pinkish-gray.

Line – The pedigree of ancestors; family tree.

Litter – The name given to a group of kittens born at the same time from a single female.

Mask – A type of coloring seen on the face in some breeds.

Matts – Knots or tangles in the cat's fur.

Mittens – White markings on the feet of a cat.

Moggie – Another name for a mixed breed cat.

Mutation – A change in the DNA of a cell.

Muzzle – The nose and jaws of an animal.

Natural Breed – A breed that developed without selective breeding or the assistance of humans.

Neutering – Desexing a male cat.

Open Show – A show in which spectators are allowed to view the judging.

Pads – The thick skin on the bottom of the feet.

Particolor – A type of coloration in which there are markings of two or more distinct colors.

Patched – A type of coloration in which there is any solid color, tabby, or tortoiseshell color plus white.

Pedigree – A purebred cat; the cat's papers showing its family history.

Pet Quality – A cat that is not deemed of high enough standard to be shown or bred.

Piebald – A cat with white patches of fur.

Points – Also color points; markings of contrasting color on the face, ears, legs, and tail.

Pricked – Referring to ears that sit upright.

Purebred – A pedigreed cat.

Queen – An intact female cat.

Roman Nose – A type of nose shape with a bump or arch.

Scruff – The loose skin on the back of a cat's neck.

Selective Breeding – A method of modifying or improving a breed by choosing cats with desirable traits.

Senior – A cat that is more than 5 but less than 7 years old.

Sire – The male parent of a cat.

Solid – Also self; a cat with a single coat color.

Spay – Desexing a female cat.

Stud – An intact male cat.

Tabby – A type of coat pattern consisting of a contrasting color over a ground color.

Tom Cat – An intact male cat.

Tortoiseshell – A type of coat pattern consisting of a mosaic of red or cream and another base color.

Tri-Color – A type of coat pattern consisting of three distinct colors in the coat.

Tuxedo – A black and white cat.

Unaltered – A cat that has not been desexed.

Index

H

I

J

K

L

M

N

Photo Credits

Page 1 Photo by user Zkittler via Pixabay.com,

https://pixabay.com/en/devon-rex-tomcat-cat-pillow-2740865/

Page 7 Photo by user Nickolas Titkov via Flickr.com,

https://www.flickr.com/photos/titkov/5289172567/

Page 17 Photo by user Nickolas Titkov via Flickr.com,

https://www.flickr.com/photos/titkov/15983246306/

Page 36 Photo by user Andreas-photography via Flickr.com,

https://www.flickr.com/photos/sheepies/4694399920/

Page 49 Photo by user Nickolas Titkov via Flickr.com,
https://www.flickr.com/photos/titkov/5289777648/

Page 56 Photo by user joan!ta via Flickr.com,

https://www.flickr.com/photos/heartbeats/10756033424/

Page 61 Photo by user Quinn Dombrowski via Flickr.com,

https://www.flickr.com/photos/quinnanya/5432351283/

Page 70 Photo by user joan!ta via Flickr.com,

https://www.flickr.com/photos/heartbeats/20759905029/

References

5 Things You Didn't Know About the Devon Rex -
IHeartCats.com
https://iheartcats.com/5-things-you-didnt-know-about-the-devon-rex/

About the Devon Rex – Cats Fancier Association
http://cfa.org/Breeds/BreedsCJ/DevonRex.aspx

Cats 101: Devon Rex – Animal Planet
https://www.animalplanet.com/tv-shows/cats-101/videos/devon-rex

Devon Rex – Cattime.com
http://cattime.com/cat-breeds/devon-rex-cats

Devon Rex – Wikipedia.org
https://en.wikipedia.org/wiki/Devon_Rex

Devon Rex at a glance – Hillspet.com
https://www.hillspet.com/cat-care/cat-breeds/devon-rex

Devon Rex Kitten Care Sheet – DevonRexCats.net
http://devonrexcats.net/Wisecracks-Devon-Rex-Breeder-New-Zealand-Devon-Rex-Kitten-Care-Sheet.html

Get to Know the Devon Rex: A Social and Curious Cat Breed – Catster.com
http://www.catster.com/cats-101/get-to-know-the-devon-rex-a-social-and-curious-cat-breed

Kitten Shopping List – DevonRexCats.com
http://devonrexcats.net/Wisecracks-Devon-Rex-Breeder-New-Zealand-Getting-Ready-For-Your-Devon-Rex-Kitten.html

Pet Parent's Guide to Devon Rex Training – PetsWorld.in
https://www.petsworld.in/blog/devon-rex-training.html

What Foods to Feed Your New Devon Rex – Animal Care Tip
http://animalcaretip.com/what-foods-to-feed-your-new-devon-rex/

Feeding Baby
Cynthia Cherry
978-1941070000

Axolotl
Lolly Brown
978-0989658430

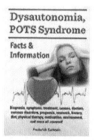

Dysautonomia, POTS
Syndrome
Frederick Earlstein
978-0989658485

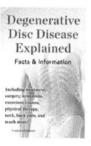

Degenerative Disc
Disease Explained
Frederick Earlstein
978-0989658485

Sinusitis, Hay Fever,
Allergic Rhinitis Explained
Frederick Earlstein
978-1941070024

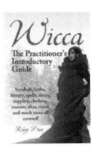

Wicca
Riley Star
978-1941070130

Zombie Apocalypse
Rex Cutty
978-1941070154

Capybara
Lolly Brown
978-1941070062

Eels As Pets
Lolly Brown
978-1941070167

Scabies and Lice Explained
Frederick Earlstein
978-1941070017

Saltwater Fish As Pets
Lolly Brown
978-0989658461

Torticollis Explained
Frederick Earlstein
978-1941070055

Kennel Cough
Lolly Brown
978-0989658409

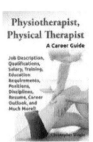

Physiotherapist, Physical
Therapist
Christopher Wright
978-0989658492

Rats, Mice, and Dormice
As Pets
Lolly Brown
978-1941070079

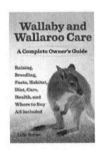

Wallaby and Wallaroo Care
Lolly Brown
978-1941070031

Bodybuilding Supplements
Explained
Jon Shelton
978-1941070239

Demonology
Riley Star
978-19401070314

Pigeon Racing
Lolly Brown
978-1941070307

Dwarf Hamster
Lolly Brown
978-1941070390

Cryptozoology
Rex Cutty
978-1941070406

Eye Strain
Frederick Earlstein
978-1941070369

Inez The Miniature Elephant
Asher Ray
978-1941070353

Vampire Apocalypse
Rex Cutty
978-1941070321